ENTERING A LIFE

ERNESTO TREJO

Entering a Life

Ernesto Trejo

This volume is made possible by a grant from the National Endowment for the Arts, a federal agency.

Arte Publico Press
University of Houston
Houston, TX 77204-2090

Acknowledgments

"It's your Name And It's Also December" was first published in *The Nation*. "Cipriana" was first published in *Partisan Review*. "This Is What Happened," "The President Is Up Before the Fruit Vendor," "The Day Of Vendors," "E. Is In Love," "E. Curses the Rich," were originally published in *Kayak*. "On Friday Nights" was first printed in *Green House*. "The Cloud Unfolding," "August," "At My Window," and "Autumn's End" first appeared in *Black Warrior Review*. "E. At the Zocalo" was first published in *Footprint Magazine*. "At My Window" and "Clouds" first appeared in *Revista Chicano-Riqueña*. "Today I'll Sit Still" first appeared in *The Antioch Review*. "One Summer" first appeared in *ZYZZYVA*. The poems "Tonight This House Speaks," "Summer," and "Waiting" first appeared in the anthology *Entrance* (Greenfield Review Press, 1975). "Entering a Life," "At Dawn," and "For Jaime Sabines" were first published in the anthology *Piecework: 19 Fresno Poets* (Silver Skates Publishing, 1987).

Trejo, Ernesto.
    Entering a Life / Ernesto Trejo.
        p.   cm.
    ISBN 1-55885-014-7
    I. Title.
    PS3570.R375E5   1990   89-77254
    811'.54--dc20   CIP

Entering a Life

For Victor and Kerry

Contents

I

One Summer

Against the elm
that spun its rumor
up and down the block
one afternoon
your bike leaned
like a drunk
among others
a pearl of sweat
on the handlebar

Your hero that summer?
The kid who climbed
the streetlights
and shattered them
one by one
with his baseball bat

Hair in the armpits
like weeds
in a vacant lot
Tyranny of tight shoes
your bones
stretching like a cat
at dawn

You bowed
to the crown of blood
your foot
pierced
by a rusty nail

you bowed to the stars
that came out

like shy students
and took their places

You bowed
to the warm shoulders
of desire
nudging you
like a brother
in the dark

August

When the sister
of your mother
woke up and blessed the day
with her one eye,
when all the pigeons
in the block
prayed in her fever,
when her toes curled
the next day
and her lamp winked,
you were there.
           A child,
you took yourself
by the hand
through everything.
This was August,
and a year later
it all came back,
the terror, when you saw
your one friend in the rain,
the mud on his cowboy boots,
also dead. You took
yourself by the hand.
             You lied
to your bicycle, the lawn
on which you played was water.
There, the eggs could hold
whales, winged horsed,
firemen in shiny suits
that might burn like ants.
             Bored,

you went in the house
and pulled the feathers
from your hat
one by one,
gave them each a name
and commanded them to sing
into the space
that once held
one of your teeth.

A Good Day

Father, one summer I was seven,
on a Sunday, the usual day
for miracles,
you held me and my brother
all afternoon
slapping the river.
Told us to open our eyes underwater
and not to be afraid. There,
I saw the current combing your legs,
small and sturdy,
the tired legs of a barber.
Later you swam where it was deep
with us clinging to your neck
until you said *let go*,
knowing that we wouldn't sink.
At dusk we drove back to town
and didn't tell you how much water
we had swallowed all day,
how we felt the slice of moon
tickling our bellies,
a barber's razor knocking softly
against your head, your profile
of stone a calm fist
against the night
and all the hands that held it.

Sunday

—for my father

Yesterday was Sunday. Your grandson
stared at your feet and found
the eclipse that moved for years
across your nails. He discovered
a callus, tapped it,
but it didn't go away.
Later, you dressed
while mother slept and went outside,
the leashed dog slightly
ahead of you. Nothing
was revealed, nothing given,
nothing for your tired feet
or the rest . . .
One by one the stars sank
into the patina of the new day,
the dog licked your feet, and
when the day opened like a mouth,
you walked in.

Like the Earth

—for my newborn son

My little one, you are finally
here. So much like the earth,
through a flower . . .
Out of the darkness, underground star,
where did you come from?
Cold space suddenly thundering
with a heartbeat.
What's in those fists?
Wrath? Happiness?
A warrior. But, where are your weapons?
Your laughter, your tears?
Like everything else in the world,
you are here flowing
like the hours.
Look at this perplexed face.
This is the face that you will wear
on the day when I become one
with the roots,
as you look over your shoulder
and see the night
swelling up in the distance,
already
a cricket
trilling in the bushes.

Cipriana

—my grandmother, *in memoriam*

1

There were trains that went in the tunnels
and never came out. The eyes of horses
focused and trotted to their deaths.
The corn slept in the cistern
and was rotted when it woke.

2

An old photo. You are next to your marigolds
(the flower of death, mother tells me)
and I cling to your skirt. How strange to be 4,
watching the print on your skirt. Behind us
the paint peeled off the wall all morning,
your honeysuckle thirsted for light, your ivy
found a crevice and went in.

3

You never saw the sea or the pelicans
winged like angels. In the end, your visions
were embarrassing: a granddaughter
sleeping with Satan; a voice in every corner,
beckoning; your husband, the blind man
lost in prayer, a daddy that would punish.
Your daughters, aging, won't talk about the end.
I do. I take the space in which you lived,
your life, and put it in my pocket, and name you.

Summer

Killed a gopher
in my garden.
Split it
with a shovel.
First I cut
only a leg.
Could have stopped
there, but
a mutilated gopher
can turn us
into what we are.
Could have done
what I did
or could have run
away, sobbing,
baring my neck
to anyone.

The morning went on,
the shovel put away,
and with the mail came news
of Grandmother at last dead,
finally joining her parents
whom she talked to every day
when she became a little girl again.
She would kiss Grandfather's hand
and rub it against her cheeks
mumbling words we couldn't make out.
Everyone smiled, embarrassed
but understanding, until
one day the kiss was a furious bite
and no one could stop the laughter

from her bloody mouth.

The Cloud Unfolding

It starts with the picture of my grandfather,
machinegunned in his car, Packard De Luxe, 1923.
A snapshot with poor composition, slightly
out of focus, it holds the forty-three
bullets that pushed for light or air
& which now find their black spaces and obey
our eyes. His last curse will never leave
this picture, his body will never
leave that car, his blood will forever
cake on the red upholstering
(Someone pulled you out of the car, someone
        else
unfolded a blanket over your face not knowing
that you wanted to see that cloud unfold
over the whole sky
or gather into rain & flood your eyes.
Your last curse gave way to visions of battle,
of other men, never yourself,
dying in the heat & the dust).
In El Paso my grandfather once stayed up
all night & when the sun rose he shaved the goa-
        tee,
tapped over his heart & felt the fake passport.
Later he emerged from the hotel a businessman,
like Lenin, & walked six blocks to the train sta-
        tion,
a black mushroom in the fog,
a piece of shit under the sky of El Paso
or Geneva, a sky that ate his shirts & sucked
his head into a chisel of anger.
Further back, in one autumn the Eiffel went up,

a symbol of itself, & every washerwoman
felt proud of her city
(But one night, in 1936, the tower would crack,
collapsing over Los Angeles, against the pave-
    ment
dressed with spit & yellow newspapers
that told the Negroes *Burn, Generation of Vipers*
& the Mexicans *Go Back Where You Came From*.
Roosevelt, the syphilitic Jew, will sell
to the Germans tomorrow at 10:15. My father
is in his kitchen, dropping ice cubes in a glass
of water, when the phone rings & a man
tells him that his bar is in flames.
When my father arrives at the bar, nine years
of good luck go up in smoke & someone tells
    him
it was the Negroes, your brother refused them
    credit.
My father nods, not knowing why, & stands
there for hours following the slow cloud from
    his bar
until the sun silhouettes the church two blocks
    away
& he thinks *that shadow is a bad omen*).
Father, for the rest of your life, in Mexico,
you never mentioned the fire
but spoke of flappers, of Roosevelt, of Chaplin
devoured by a clock on his way to work.

A Death In the Family

I was off to Los Angeles to the burial of my cousin. The drive, as usual, was tedious, except for the sunset in the mountains and the stops to sip coffee from the thermos bottle.

The Nicaraguan deacon asked: May I have your permission to address you in Spanish? I want to speak to Brother Ezequiel in my tongue. Less than one out of four understood the question, since it was posed in Spanish, let alone the sermon that followed, starring Lazarus. What a cruel joke to address a corpse on Lazarus risen from the dead. Then he went on and on about "Brother" Ezequiel not really being dead.

The sermon was still floating in the air when I walked up to view the coffin. The gruesome face of death gave nothing back. The pitiful face of death made me feel pitiful and gave me not a sense of brevity, but of the ridiculousness of my self-importance. The face of death snickers at us from the faces of the dead. The living who are scrutinized, the living who have to answer questions. The living who stare blankly at each other before the corpse of a loved one and think, "Hell, it could have been me ... "

But it was Ezequiel, my father's nephew, who forty years before had been entrusted to him and his new bride for three years; who at 13 broke another boy's arm for ridiculing his soft R's. When I met him, in the 50's, he had five children of his own, was settled in the life of Mexican-American-blue-collar Whittier. Still, the up-

turned smile, the kid's glint in the eyes. I saw
him then as the epitomy of style, his black hair
fluttering in the wind as he rode his Harley. But
these are *my* memories, the events as I saw them.

In the end, Ezequiel was consumed, fragile, what
little hair left gone gray. Oh, the indignity of
death after a long cobalt treatment! It was a
good thing that Father wasn't there. The next
morning there was a woman who wailed so loud-
ly that I felt she desecrated the last few minutes
of the burial. She was wife number 3. She had
been up all night on cigarettes and coffee, for
the last three days ... But I found dignity in his
children. Eddie, Ernie, Ricky, Terry. And Vir-
gie, my age, looking haggard, exuded wisdom in
her calm beauty. They are now older than Eze-
quiel was when I met him.

There is a country in the mind, made of other
times and places. Ezequiel wanders on his mo-
torcycle and toasts his memories of Mexico. In
that republic I am nine, with a wisdome seldom
again matched, for I knew by then the elusive-
ness of time and space, but also the strength of
memory, for my best friend had just died in the
rain, and I had looked death in the eye, and that
night dreamed that he winked back, a last good-
bye.

This time there was no winking back. There was
a man lowered in a coffin to wander off in the
thick waters of death, and dozens of relatives
milling around, grieving or absent-minded, I
don't know which. And there I was, attending
a funeral for the second time in my life.

Entering a Life

Once I was in love & I think I loved that girl
much more than she loved me. Would I heal?
    Would I
appear once in her dreams robed in yellow light
    as
an omen of truth? In the frailty of love I re-
    sented her.
Had she equaled the intensity of my longing I
    could have
imagined our bodies as one single lovely beast
roaming ... & if this beast died the next day its
    death
would not matter. I remember that when I was
    12
I heard about an uncle who twenty years before
had gone away for good. But he hadn't died
like his younger brother, whose life was taken
    slowly
by TB. My uncle who disappeared simply stopped
writing home, stopped sending money & post-
    cards
from exotic places: Los Angeles, Pittsburgh,
Des Moines ... They wondered where you went,
    uncle Felix.
The story about you entered my life, a distant
airplane that got closer until it really meant noth-
    ing
between two people talking; they just talk louder
& as the airplane disappears in the sky their voices
subside. No one looks up.
You, Felix, the extrovert, the handsome one, the

dancer,
the one who talked to children, dazzled the girls
    & had
the quiet respect of men, could have saved them.
    This
I could tell in their envy & admiration & their
quiet resentment that grew like fingernails.
You could have linked them to the world & to
    each other
& for that their lives could have been different.
    Instead,
they sought spirits & became thieves, liars, con-
    verts to
anything, whorehouse keepers, solid citizens.
Had you died for real, they could have gone on,
    & someone
would have said in hushed tones at family gath-
    erings,
"Felix ... Poor soul. He died so young ... "
    They could have
taken turns at it. Instead, you entered their lives
for a short time, a companion at the movies who
    leaves
his seat & never returns, while they all sit there,
    waiting,
until the theater closes & they are ushered out.
Two years after your letters stopped someone
    saw
you in Missouri, tending desk at a motel
on the outskirts of a town with an unpronounce-
    able name.
I pictured you behind the counter, not really
noticed by the young man who fills out the reg-
    ister,

the bulge on his pants breathing with a life of its
   own.
When the young man & his girl walk up to their
   room their laughter stays in the air for a few
   seconds & then enters slowly
the worn rug. You turn around & continue read-
   ing a book,
your back bent like the tall grass across the high-
   way, or
like your life. Later, someone said you were do-
   ing time
in El Paso for smuggling workers. You appeared
   then
defiant in a quiet way, a little fortune stashed
   away
for your release, keeping to yourself.
Years later, someone swore you were in Chicago,
   portly
& happy, the owner of a jewelry store. I said to
   myself,
Why Not? You would wear thick glasses & a
   three-piece suit,
speak in low tones & seldom smile, for it would
   be
a quiet business, the thick carpet drowning out
   your steps.
Another time it was you in the hospital in San
   Jose,
a broken back, another casualty of the apricot
   season.
I imagined you craving morphine, while the young
   nurses
gathered in the next room for coffee & talked
of boyfriends going off to war, of disease enter-

ing
their children, of boredom eating up their youth.
These stories went on for years, even after your
        parents died
& your brothers & sisters were scattered around
like bruised fruit.
Uncle, after 20 years of stories I know so little.
        I want
to imagine you content, honoring your name. I
        want you
falling in love once with a girl whose love
matched the intensity of yours. I see you bois-
        terous &
the two of you drunk with love for a few years.
Until one day she runs off with a lover & leaves
        you
with two daughters whom you raise. Years pass
& you are left a little less happy & unsure
of everything & ashamed at being shortchanged.
        Or maybe
you felt belittled & didn't care & changed your
        name
& invented a past to tell your daughters,
just as I am inventing your life now because I no
        longer
want to hear stories or obituaries about you.
I don't want you to be a ghost
disturbing lives that had nothing to do with yours,
even if at one time they called you brother, son.

II

This Is What Happened

—for Gary Soto

I

This is what happened:
She refused to lean on my shoulder
and it hurt. The sky
was empty and the radio said good night.
The mountains around us were teasing:
At times I thought we had been
devoured. At times it seemed
they had vanished.
I fondled the rabbit's foot
on the keychain and felt it tick.
Ahead I saw a tumbleweed
with a thousand tiny eyes.
I saw a porcupine or a possum leap
from behind the wild eyes.
I swerved the car and lost control
of the situation.

II

This is what happened:
You never lost control. We hit
a wild pig before sundown and you said
it was unfortunate and mused on probability.
We stopped.
The sun was sinking behind,
and darkness was moving on us, kicking
tumbleweeds, blowing sand.
We held hands and drove
into the darkness. The radio said good night

and I leaned on your shoulder.
I always lean on your shoulder.
You hummed an old song and I fell asleep.
You kept humming so you wouldn't.
You forgot the words and made some up. You
were confident. You knew
I would die that night, yet you were confident.
You opened my door and swerved the car
at the curve. There were no animals.
There was only me on the shoulder of the road.
My body a still river, my head on a lagoon.
You thought you saw a swallow,
a black swallow, and still you didn't lose control.
The mountain to your left collapsed
and I leaped on you, where I have been
ever since, lodged somewhere,
between your neck and your shoulder.

At My Window

At my window, I write:
Three children in the swings
testing how high they can go,
how much the chains will hold.

I imagine this April air
humming in their throats,
the trees behind them
disappearing like ice.
Off to one side
a younger kid awaits his turn
and pats the ground while his mouth
opens in a cry or a yawn.

Today I feel like that kid.
Last night I opened my arms
to embrace my muted dreams
and when I awoke I went around
shutting every door and window.

Nothing will happen. The sky
will go on circling above.
The trees will dig deeper.
In this corner of the planet, with
an angle of sunlight on my shoulder,
my pencil tucked away,
I stand up and leave.

You

This morning, for no reason at all,
I thought of you.
There's no mystery here.
You've been a tiny lump in my throat
all these years,
making house in the dark.

I imagine you in your other house,
posted behind the kitchen window,
waiting for your children
to step off the bus
and come to you, hungry.
A minute ago
you stumbled in and out of rooms,
looking for a way out.
But it was raining outside
and you too were hungry.

Your Room

Your room would only be complete
with music and a tired cat,

a phone pleading
and no hand to lift it.

From the window, a sidewalk
lined with willows would stretch on.

On the wall, a map of the city
would peek from behind your back.

Under the table,
a pair of battered boots, your size.

You will hear sycamore leaves
breaking like glass.

Your wrists will join like palms,
like the murmur crossing your life.

Window Washer

It's always August.
Before sunup
he leaves the scaffold
and enters the world
of office workers:
the raffles of forms,
the committees
of pencils,
the muted staples.

Now he is free to let
the typewriters hum
their one song,
the ink scribble
its signature on the wall.
He dances to the window
with bundles of paper,
my babies, and watches
how they shower
onto the street.
By the window,
he strikes a conversation
with the hanging ferns:
they speak
of how they got
to this place,
of the stars
who basically are
like children,
of the clock
whose heart is dark.
They confess

their wish of following
the air, of burning
with the fire in the East
while the typewriters
hum and hum
the only song they know.

In Short

Let's say that on the corner there is a man.
That today his son spread out his arms
in a dream in which he never woke
and this man saw in his son a bird
but wasn't sure if the wings spread out to fly
or if, being in the air,
he would spiral into his arms.

Let's say that underneath this man
the grass is crowned by thorns,
and on these you can see mosquitoes
swallowing air and the air
is nothing but a backround or a synthesis
of the scene; let's say a painter
imagined the whole thing up.

Let's say, in short, that there's no painter,
but there is a child, a man ... maybe a painter,
and they are in different cities and today
they have gathered in my house, at my table,
and I didn't toy with their fate;
but described something that didn't happen in
        my poem,
but in a city the name of which I ignore.

On Friday Nights

On Friday nights I go to the bakery two blocks away and talk to the woman behind the counter. When the customers leave, she moves around pretending not to see me, which signals that it is time to put on my act. I will talk too much or not at all, I'll pretend to be a salesman, a customer shopping for a birthday cake, a detective taking fingerprints, or a blind man who has lost his cane.

She smiles, unimpressed.

Sometimes she will join in the act when customers walk in, like the time when, pretending I had fainted, she let a woman smear perfume on my nose and an old man slap my face. One time I pinched her infinite ass and explained I was shopping for watermelons. Isn't this the supermarket?

I know that when I leave she writes down who I have been and has a grading scale of 1 to 100. Late at night, walking home I feel relieved. It's over, but who will I be next week?

Dear Son Letter

Dear son I have to explain some things first of all I am not crazy but you would have me and the world belive otherwise insanity not even momentarily has ever infected me where do you get those ideas was I mean to your daughters I owe you no apologies you are my son and must understand I am a poor old woman trying to make things easy I live well by myself and am happy people like you enjoy playing martyr (poor mother is losing her marbles) and I can go along with that game but only if it works for me so we aren't fooling anybody if you think I am the way I am because I need love well I got news for you I don't and I don't think anybody does what is important is that you know that the only thing I look forward to an old woman my age abandoned like an old couch is to have your two precious daughters with me two weeks next month I promise they won't get scared in the dark if they come I think it is within your power to make them understand how much a lonely old woman needs companionship at times.

To the Child Dead In My Larynx

Since morning I've been at a burial.
I dressed this boy like an angel
and took away his name. Cussed him out
and snatched away his parents. Kicked him
in the ass to prove that I'm here.

I would spill off his shoulders like grease,
he would be a zoo staring me down.
And what do we share? He gave
birth to me: I buried him
with fresh dirt and spit.

He's always shooting rings of smoke,
promises floating to heaven.
I'm a tundra where he wanders
carrying flesh under his arm.
Would he let me break in like light
through his eyelids? Would he be
a story to feed my big bones?
Would he come around to show me
the lint inside his pockets?

I Will Tell You

I will tell you, Alighieri,
why yesterday you couldn't write.
Long ago, in Bologna, at Mama
Luisa's brothel you mocked
your professor, his theological
shortcomings. The sun
gathered in the cup
of the elm
and then was gone. Then
you envied no one,
not the bishop who's been
pregnant for ten years,
not the Pope
or the ring of gnats
over his head.
Later, your cat purred
and fell asleep
and you thought of her dreams.
Beyond the Alps,
smelling of money, the wind
was born in Venice.
Maybe tonight
you can tell the world
how pride was erased
from your forehead.

Because

I spilled the coins
from my mouth and called it quits
before, you may think of me
as a fraud, a fanatic enemy
of horoscopes. Darkness frightens
me, but friend,
it's nothing like the light
which can pierce through
taking it all. You can read this:
my fear, my awe, the fall
from light into flame,
my own ignorance finding a path
with words and theology.
My life is the River Arno
approaching the sea.
Am I like the wind that bends
the wheat fields into submission
or am I the stalk of wheat
carving a small place in the air?

All These Years

the lord of Ravenna
has been kind.
What was my secret?
Water, fire.
Philosophy and my memories
of Florence.
Of course I have
another life. A wife,
children who have joined
the academicians
in deciphering my verses.
I befriended scholars,
took short trips,
locked myself up
and grew weaker
struggling with my visions.
Bitter, a biographer
will say fifty years
hence, and that will be
that, Beatrice.

My Tongue Is the Tongue

of Italian women
who squeeze eggplants
at market; tongues that can feel
a man like a canker sore,
a jewel.
      Tongue
of shepherds, dry
like the tongues of their sheep,
circling
the steep embankments
of the river.

The Streets Held

everyone all night
and what flickered were not lights
but people like yourself,
their dreams reduced to night air.

You followed a bird before it dove
into a tree, followed the woman who paused
before a lamp that pointed skyward,
a star that signaled to another star.

E. At the Zocalo

At the small zocalo,
sipping beer and bored:
sunlight was a fading scribble
in the West, the heat was ascending
like a saint, the empty streets
going nowhere, the signs urging no one,
the droopy leaves like rags.

I'm not sure. Maybe all that silence
spilled out of the church, maybe
the blank sky, suspended,
was the stillness of my life and
that moment was the many afternoons
in the dead center of the wheel.

Then, first on the highest cross,
then on the eaves, on the unused balconies,
on the trees and the telephone lines:
the sparrows and their flapping
filled the little world of the zocalo.
A clouded wing or a black cape
coming finally to rest?

I don't know what followed. Maybe
they kept raining down like stones; maybe
the silence was only inside;
maybe the sparrows were dust in the air,
stars, the black gloves of happiness,
the speech of God.
Or maybe, you know, they were sparrows,
because hours later when the East ignited
and caught on fire they left again

in silence for the fields
and I stood up and left that bench
to warm up my hands, to pour some coffee
over them, to make them come to see
as eyes: not to obey and sit still like hands.

E. Gives a Name

Later, no one knew who named him.
No one cared, and the name
blended with his face in the mirror
and the springs under his chair
repeated it over dinner.
He wore it the way one wears a scar
or a mole. He wore it
until it was no more
than a taste in his mouth
that he couldn't wash out.

I nicknamed him. I christened him
Worm. Later, it was the link
between us: my guilt, his hate.
He would dream of getting back,
but a nickname never caught,
not even in his head. If he said,
snail, moth, spider, scorpion,
these would become slimy, winged
eight-legged words, meant for me
but ringing in his head
like the clear bell of his childhood.

Some nights he would dream
of everyone sobbing in repentance,
dream the sparrow landing on his finger
and flying off with his nickname.
He saw the cockroach on its back
kicking and dying like a name,
he walked to the window and saw
the darkness stretching like a yawn
and wakened, and awake he went

to the mirror and the name was there,
blended with his face. The name was also
in his throat, a bitter taste
that he couldn't wash out.
The name was all around him:
it was the air
he was breathing to stay alive.

E. Is In Love

What fire glows under her skirt! What
sparrow is gnawing at his heart!
The April air is slapping him
all the way home, the stupid trees
running after the awkward poem
circling his heart.
The stars are dust on the table
his dry throat is asking . . .

Go on, stupid heart, go on loving her.
Everything you do speaks like a mouth,
though you have nothing to say.
You wake up to words—table,
lipstick, balcony hanging like a tongue,
flower pot—objects, humble
like your heart: it's the world
that shouts her name!

The moon—tedium under his pillow.
The night—sprouting like a fountain.
His car—a matchbook holding its breath.
People—dry sticks poking through water.
The streets—question marks pointing nowhere.
His body, his living body, his blood
like ink & the pulley going crazy . . .

E. Curses the Rich

San Teodulo, give them vinegar when they thirst.
Holy Peter, when they hunger, look the other
way.
St. Frigid, if they bleed, have some salt on hand.
John the Baptist, drown them.
Blessed Caldron of St. Ursula, bubble in their
ears.
St. Joseph the Good—one day they'll eat your
sandals.
Dogs of St. Blas, feast on their throats.
Bats of the Apparition, shriek forever in their
dreams.
Emmanuel, Son of God, spit in the eyes that
have never seen.
And you, Holy Horse of Bethlehem, rage of the
poor,
kick their heads into the solid wall of money
that froze their hearts.

The Arch Of the Sky Dream

1.

Swallows crown the afternoon.
Your eyes reflected on a silver spoon
make you sob.
You take pictures of the sun.
A woman with whose voice
you fell in love
has been waiting for years.
Amorous cats descend to their alley.
A butcher wanders in the forest
under the eyeful watch of vultures.
A cop sails off on a boat full of rats.
A white monkey swims a white river.
The shadow of a blind man drowns.
All the streetlights tumble in the rain.
Two lovers go on kissing long
after their mouths begin to bleed.
And what do the nervous leaves know?
All morning long a spider waited
in a vineyard and no one came.
A truck hauled away all the drunks.
Three kids, bleeding at the elbows
and looking for gold coins,
rip open the belly of a goat.
Bats fly off with the hermit's eyes.
A rapist sits still in the park.
A boy is grinning from inside
the foggy windows of your car.

2.

One day you want to cover
the arch of the sky
the way a raven does,
the way a finger can.
Then you are reduced to an itch
that moves around your chest.
Today you are your soul,
a misprint in a book
no one will open anymore.
You shout at the ears of God,
but they are sewn shut
with a silk thread
that leads to a tired heart.

The day leaned against
the door for a while,
then on your hand,
and it was gone.
This sky has been watching
you, going off to work,
coming home, not strong,
nor tired, nor anything.
It listened to your arguments
patiently, bored, or deaf,
a blackened orange
suspended
in the frozen air.

The first stars appear,
and you are their shepherd
leading them to the troughs
of the coming dawn.
You are leaving home,

clumps of dirt
under your shoes.
The geranium
that exploded this morning
in a burst of laughter
goes away quietly too
under a dry climate
of stars.

III

At Dawn

The spirit surges among branches.
The nervous laughter of blackbirds
traces a dagger over the day's flesh.

*

To an assembly of birds on a wire,
plums below fill with their dark milk
and the shadow of a small cloud sizzles.

*

Two stars still burn:
eyes about to go out:
Another blind day.

Clouds

At dawn
they are
huge peaches
on the bare trees
All day
they act
like the lost
or else
they approach us
asking
At night
they reflect
something like smoke
in the heart
that confuses
a pistol
for an eye
Later
exhausted
they rest
like us
waiting
for the moment
of parting
like eyelids

Autumn Postcards

An arrowhead of birds heading South.
On a Greyhound bus, field workers
huddle at the rear and lip-synch
to their shiny radios.

*

At the bottom of a dry canal,
among tires, beer cans, a shopping cart,
a child's lost ball, shoes, lamps,
what-nots, I saw the body of a woman,
impatient, like a Buick stuck in traffic.

It's Your Name and
It's Also December

—after Aridjis

It's your name and it's also December
the last lights of the town blank out
like the pulse that climbs two churches
and stops
I watch you fall asleep
and find you
not the hunter but the deer
find you
a patch of flowers
on a terrace facing the white sea
winter without end
in other cities men rise
in other dreams cities rise nameless
a brook forks when your fingers part
or else the procession of the wind
pauses before your fingers
it's the spaces between stars
the quiet march of the sun
lying in ambush
it's the words that stop squealing
what skin isn't bare
what fist doesn't pound on a wall
it's the snow blowing through every garden
entering every house

2 A.M.

Under the covers, the winds of sleep
rock the poppies of your breasts
We close our eyes to this life
and open them to the other Next to the eager-
    ness of the fly, the wrath
of a flock of sparrows
and the saintliness of the horse
you fall off the precipice of the day's bridge
The teeth of winter
also sleep for a while
Under the bed, my shoes too rest
their burning eyes
At 2 A.M. God comes out to stretch his legs
and lights the cigarette of a whore
that struts in front of the drugstore
The plank of solitude
that spawns fraternities
—snake and hare, owl and mouse—
is dispelled when I exist in your dream
alongside with whom I was and will be
The night is a knife of diving dust
You arch a shoulder and office buildings collapse
when your knees point skyward
there's thunder in a desert
If you were to open your eyes now
you could mangle a continent

Red

One time
the whole world wore red.
Flowerpots, earth, blood, flesh.
Red water sifted through red earth.
Perplexed birds filled their beaks
with dirt-red air; I saw them
through red irises, and beyond
a heaven carved out of sulphur.
Red—the beginning, veins, the sun's lament.
Red—crabs, their hungry pincers.
The wisdom of the heart is red.
Red was for *Stop, don't do it*.
The dust on the roadside was red
and the first star that winked
was a premonition of the scratch
of a paw upon my hand.

Tonight This House Speaks

Tonight this house speaks to me
through the creaking in the cupboards
and the refrigerator's humming.
Believe me, when this house shakes
under my feet
it isn't because of the train.
There's something in the basement.
I don't know what, I've never been there,
I'm afraid of the empty room
that leads to it.

Tonight I'm a hearing machine.
Beer bottles are crashing
in the dusty corners.
Even the spiders
are hesitant.
The crack in the ceiling
is a fissure in the brain
for all I know,
this kidney ache might be a sign
of rusty pipes, the cricket's
clicking has been the song
of my ventricles
all these years.

Thank God the water goes on at 2.
Then I sleep
while the plum tree drinks on,
a water full of sounds.

Waiting

Still dark. I don't trust
the newspaper that ignores me.
"The accused murderer had
a disturbed childhood."
I shouldn't worry. As I
think this the noise
of dogs rummaging
through garbage cans
takes over.
By now they've found
the canary who came down
with pneumonia over the weekend
and ended up among Sunday's
chicken bones.

I return to float
on my newspaper
and imagine
someday I will understand
electricity.

Sunlight barely filters
through the sycamores
and the Angelus covers it all.

What is real is the praying mantis
on my porch, sucking at the life
that the lightbulb refuses to give,
it's the two flies I will find
on my cactus, the absent-minded killer,
it's the neckties rousing from sleep
in the racks of *The Emporium* and *Pucci's*

waiting nervously for their masters.

Autumn's End

It begins when the TV mentions the name of my
    street,
saying in passing that the woman next door has
    died.
Yes, the one whose name I never knew, the name
that even now escapes me. I will watch
the leaves from her ash trees pile up all winter.

Now deer start to come down from the high coun-
    try
to a place between snow and this valley lost in
    fog.
And my shaggy dog scuttles between rooms.

Then there's the ants. When winter stumbles on
    them
they go under into their caves, tunnels,
and immense corridors.
And what happened to mosquitoes? Where have
    they gone
with all the blood collected?

Now there's a long peace in corners and base-
    ments
where we won't dare to step in,
black widows nest there with their young.
Outside my window a few leaves hang on.
Doubting so many things I wait for winter.
Watergrass is sprouting everywhere, even on the
    ground
where the nameless woman hides from winter.

Today I'll Sit Still

Today I'll sit still.
When my dog shuffles over and offers me
his fleas and his soul, I'll turn away.
To everything I'll close my eyes,
slice the darkness and eat it.
I'll refuse to give money on a platter
or a wet kiss under the moon.
Today I'll just sit
and say *No* to everyone and everything.
To the book on my desk, it's sad tale
of abandonment, remorse and death;
I'll keep it on the tip of my tongue
like a lukewarm dime.
No to the daily mail with its greasy fingers,
no to the telephone and its humming
through the carcass of a sparrow,
no to every projection of the self.
No to me, this preposterous accident
who speaks of the "self."
Today I'll be anti-social.
Today I'll grow into myself, be the river
of my blood, the sky inside my eyes,
the maze of my ribs, the dust that settles
on my heart. I'll let my bones sink
like pebbles in a pond.
I'll let my feet grow roots and be an extra zero
on the checks that I'll refuse to write.

On a Birthday

I learn one thing:
death is no longer
remote. It happens
to people that I love.
An aunt collapses
with a thud.
Her heart gives out
like a battered fighter.
An uncles's life
drains out
like the light of this day.
Something like the feet
of mice
scuttles in the dark corridors
of my cousin's throat.

Bodies crumble.
The earthworm's appetite ...
Only the earth does not suffer.
Today, as death came
and sat by my side
questions poured out
from the eyes of my dead
like so many snowflakes.

Some Sparrows

Lately, I've been watching them, pecking
furiously at the ground,
then retreating into the eucalyptus,
where they stagger like compasses
before their tiny hearts quit and they drop,
stone-like.
      Sometimes my cat
will sniff them and jerk back
as if pierced on the nose by a needle.
In the dark they go on dying.
While burying them I have shoveled newspapers,
their bloody lips decayed, a child's
lucky penny, a rusted pipe
that goes nowhere, the roots of weeds
tangled like kite strings or hearts . . . .
Tonight, as if for the last time, I hold
my woman's face. Were I to die, my eyes' vaults
would crave light. When I go, place a dying spar-
    row
in my hands. My soul will find a tree to perch
    on.

The President Is Up
Before the Fruit Vendor

The president is up before the fruit vendor
and goes to bed after the bus driver.
He says: History is unfair.
If the president has a toothache, we grieve.
If he smiles, we smile.
Sometimes we think we like him and we sleep
happy for it. But once we are asleep
it's different. He worries
and makes laws about our dreams.
We may not dream in other languages.
We may not dream about a life without him.
We may not dream if he's out of the country.
But there are ways . . .
We dream while we work and while we eat.
When we smile at him and shake his hand,
we're dreaming. Sometimes we see his picture
and dream of his glasses streaked with blood,
his chin tunneled by worms. Around the mouth
that punishes and forgives a string of flies
silences what could be a last word. Below,
his chest is covered with the spit of children.
Since we have never seen his eyes
we don't dream about them; they are windows
that send their black light into our hearts.

For Jaime Sabines

Even God has called it a day.
The streets of Tuxtla are empty
like the bottles of white rum
after the party.
Crickets hum discreetly.
It is so quiet.
When the dead come out
and hush secrets in the ears of young girls
their nightgowns rustle toward the fields
where oxen stumble among the high grasses.

Maybe tonight some peasants have met death
in their sleep.
Maybe their bodies will be offered
to the vultures tomorrow
and it won't matter,
for in this country no one is sure
of anything.
In this country it is best to get drunk
and forget.

And you are almost drunk,
almost sure that your hands sprouted moles,
and think of your brother and the dark
river of blood between you.
But these things don't exist
in your poems.

Who said life would be easy?
Put out your cigarette.
Drench yourself in the hot, moist night,
like a star, adrift and hopeless.

Near an Air Force Base

August. 105 in the shade.
In a field we watch the bombers
taking off and landing.
The heat over the valley
is a virus going slowly
about its business.
We sit on a fence. Between us
and these monsters the lust
of cattle is rampant and holy.
A jack rabbit ponders
its every move.
To get here we passed old houses,
a chemical plant, a toy factory.
America is busy, says Ray,
sixtyish, veteran of the zoot suit,
and now an expert at judging
perfect take-offs.
Sergio, our irreverent philosopher,
can predict the bombers'
timing and routines.
Someone said, "When the war comes,
Hell, these babies can make it
to Hawaii and be back for lunch."
Someone else said, "No, they'll bomb
Siberia and there will be
a pack of Wheaties
under the pilot's seat."
But soon our talk comes to nothing.
We came because for years
tongues of flame for fields
and villages went out from here,

the pilots high on pills
and reefer.
We came because the mind remembers,
the spirit hungers,
the body aches.

The Day Of Vendors

—for Philip Levine

Before dawn I called for you,
my poem, but you didn't come.
I had woken up to the song

of the cardinal perched
on the fence. You weren't
at my desk in all the words

that I wrote down and crossed out.
You weren't in my shoes nor in the letters
that had come and gone all month,

nor in the space held by my window,
its fourteen trees, its seven stars
that always lag behind.

All the roads of my eyes
would have plunged my brain or stumbled
out like light to look for you.

So I stepped out like a drunk
and pissed long and yellow in the ditch
and watched the steam rise slowly.

Soon the day of vendors
would begin. They would come
trumpeting new leather soles,

searching out dull knives, announcing
continents of apples and the faith
that burns in old radios.

Vegetable carts with ants

hiding under full crates and tired horses
leading them would come.

Maybe you too would come. Having
woken up to the song of a bird
whose name I knew, I said nothing

to myself, and with the spider,
the numb bee, the cat mirrored
in water, I bowed.

Poem

The night dances
in the flight
of the moth

The cactus exhales
the moon
inhales and to this
there is no end

The waters of desire
are restless

ACZ 2284   8/7/96

ENTERING A LIFE

ERNESTO TREJO

Ernesto Trejo is a poet of mysteries and incarnations, of secret unnamed presences, of the magical interior spaces of childhood and the luminous floating world that flares and throbs, that burns in time. His poems struggle to defy nothingness and death by recreating other lives, by letting other stories enter into his own story, by seeking communion with the lost and marginal, the otherwise forgotten, by witnessing, imagining, and remembering. The dark impassioned poems of *Entering a Life* are wholly alive to the Whitmanian imperative: "Who touches this, touches a man."

—Edward Hirsch

Ernesto Trejo's poetry is filled with an extraordinary exuberance and vitality. These are poems of enormous humor and wisdom. Poignant, compelling, and vibrant in their imagery, Ernesto Trejo's poems enfold us in realities that are both magical and luminous. These poems are like our fondest, wildest dreams—those which suddenly speak to us with the diamond-edged voice of true experience.

—David St. John

Trejo is a poet of conjecture, a story teller of *let's say ..., one summer ..., this is what happened ...* He writes with great invention a long-lined, ambitious poem as well as a short, refined lyric. In both instances, it's evident that he cares about his subjects, namely family, friends, childhood in Mexico and his adult years the United States, the everyday life he carves for himself, and that often romantic but shadowy figure he calls "E." Trejo has published sparingly over the years, and his first book in English is one we can learn from.

—Gary Soto

Ernesto Trejo teaches creative writing at Fresno City College.

ISBN 1-55885-014-7

Arte Publico Press
University of Houston
Houston, TX 77204-2090

COVER DESIGN MARK PIÑÓN